TOOLS FOR CAREGIVERS

- **F&P LEVEL:** C
- **WORD COUNT:** 45
- **CURRICULUM CONNECTIONS:** senses, touch, opposites

Skills to Teach

- **HIGH-FREQUENCY WORDS:** a, I, it, my, the, with
- **CONTENT WORDS:** bumpy, cold, feels, floor, fur, hands, hard, rock, sand, smooth, snow, soft, touch, tree, warm
- **PUNCTUATION:** periods
- **WORD STUDY:** long /e/, spelled ee *(feels, tree)*; long /e/, spelled y *(bumpy)*; /oo/, spelled oo *(smooth)*; long /o/, spelled ow *(snow)*
- **TEXT TYPE:** information report

Before Reading Activities

- Read the title and give a simple statement of the main idea.
- Have students "walk" through the book and talk about what they see in the pictures.
- Introduce new vocabulary by having students predict the first letter and locate the word in the text.
- Discuss any unfamiliar concepts that are in the text.

After Reading Activities

The book showed us items that have different textures and temperatures. For example, snow feels cold and sand feels warm. Cold and warm are opposites, just like smooth and bumpy and hard and soft. What other opposites can you think of? Write the examples you think of on the board.

Tadpole Books are published by Jump!, 5357 Penn Avenue South, Minneapolis, MN 55419, www.jumplibrary.com
Copyright ©2023 Jump!. International copyright reserved in all countries. No part of this book may be reproduced in any form without written permission from the publisher.

Editor: Jenna Gleisner **Designer:** Emma Bersie

Photo Credits: GoodFocused/Shutterstock, cover; Paul Hakimata Photography/Shutterstock, 1; Purino/Shutterstock, 2tl, 10–11; koldo studio/iStock, 2tr, 12–13; Saltykova Svetlana/Shutterstock, 2ml, 6–7; JHLloyd/iStock, 2mr, 8–9; sam74100/iStock, 2bl, 4–5; Kamira/Shutterstock, 2br, 14–15; Lopolo/Shutterstock, 3; Palokha Tetiana/Shutterstock, 16tl; Hayati Kayhan/Shutterstock, 16tr; Valentyn Volkov/Shutterstock, 16bl; Arlee.P/Shutterstock, 16br.

Library of Congress Cataloging-in-Publication Data
Names: Nilsen, Genevieve, author.
Title: Touch / by Genevieve Nilsen.
Description: Minneapolis, MN: Jump!, Inc., (2023)
Series: My senses | Includes index.
Audience: Ages 3–6
Identifiers: LCCN 2022011523 (print)
LCCN 2022011524 (ebook)
ISBN 9798885240987 (hardcover)
ISBN 9798885240994 (paperback)
ISBN 9798885241007 (ebook)
Subjects: LCSH: Touch—Juvenile literature.
Classification: LCC QP451 .N55 2023 (print) | LCC QP451 (ebook) | DDC 612.8/8—dc23/eng/20220325
LC record available at https://lccn.loc.gov/2022011523
LC ebook record available at https://lccn.loc.gov/2022011524

MY SENSES

TOUCH

by Genevieve Nilsen

TABLE OF CONTENTS

Words to Know..............................2

Touch...3

Let's Review!...............................16

Index..16

WORDS TO KNOW

bumpy

cold

hard

smooth

soft

warm

It feels soft.

I touch the floor.

It feels hard.

I touch a rock.

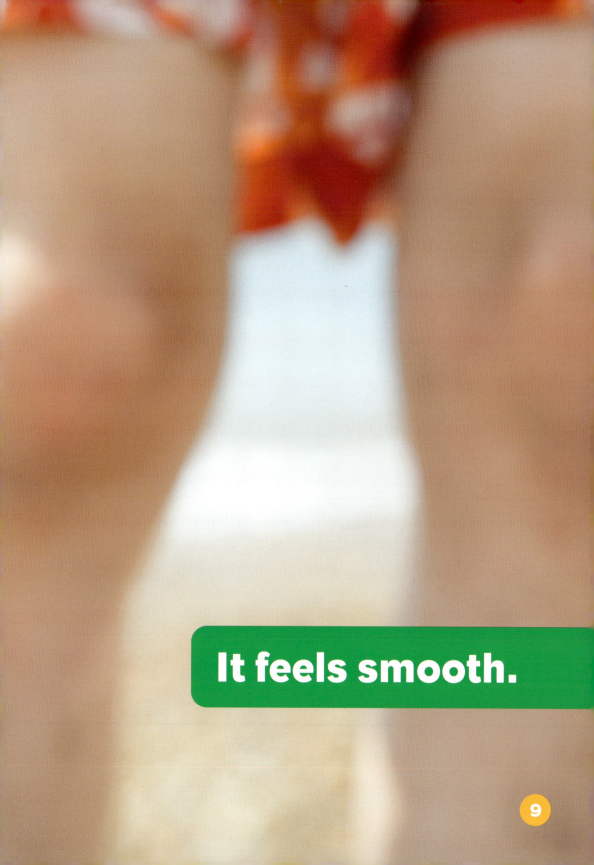
It feels smooth.

It feels bumpy.

I touch snow.

snow

It feels cold.

It feels warm.

LET'S REVIEW!

We can use our hands to touch and feel. Have you ever touched the items below? Did they feel soft, hard, smooth, bumpy, warm, or cold?

INDEX

bumpy 11

cold 13

hands 3

hard 7

smooth 9

soft 5

touch 3, 4, 6, 8, 10, 12, 14

warm 15